Grade 2.1

Decodable Practice Readers 1A - 15C
Volume 1

PEARSON Glenview, Illinois • Boston, Massachusetts
Chandler, Arizona • Hoboken, New Jersey

ISBN-13: 978-0-328-49217-6
ISBN-10:   0-328-49217-5
16 17 18 19 20 21 V0B4 18 17 16 15

UNIT 1

UNIT 2

UNIT 3

GUS

Written by Harriet Yi

Short Vowels

Ken	pet	pup	Gus	his	not	yet
six	and	got	not	big	back	quick
fun	can	run	hop	ran	tug	red
bell	tell	let	rang	did	job	well
long	jog	picnic	nap	mat	it	next
bunk	bed	pat	leg	neck	will	lick
hug						

Final -ck, -ng, -nk

back   rang   bunk   quick   long   lick

High-Frequency Words

a	his	was	he	the	then
as	is	of	to	with	

1

Ken got a pet pup.
Gus is his pup.
Ken was not yet six
and he got Gus.

2

Gus was not yet big back then.
Gus got big quick.
Gus is not yet as big as Ken.

3

Gus had fun.
Gus can run and hop.
Gus is quick.
Gus ran back.

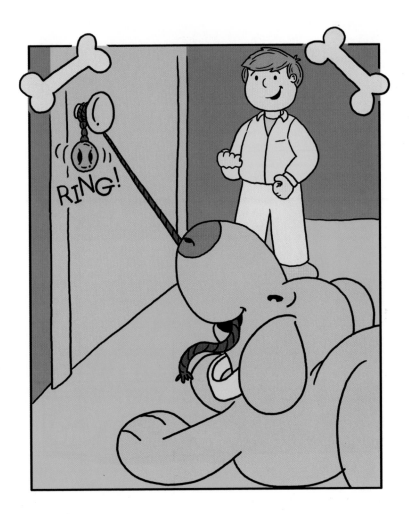

Gus can tug on his red bell.
It can tell Ken to let Gus in.
The bell rang and
Ken did his job well.

At the end of his long picnic
and jog,
Gus will nap on his mat.
It is big and red.
It is next to a bunk bed.

Ken can pat Gus on the head, leg, and neck.
Gus will lick Ken back.
Ken and Gus had fun.

Ken will hug and pet
Gus.
Ken had fun with
his big pup.

The Van

Short Vowels

Bud	had	fit	lot	in
his	van	big	rug	it
bed	got	red	basket	set
pet	tan	box	Rex	cat
not	bag	jam	ham	fan
did	yes	is	will	run
gas				

High-Frequency Words

to	a	his	he
the	was	is	

Bud had to fit a lot in his van.
He fit a big rug in it.
Bud fit his big bed in it.

Bud got a big red basket.
He set a pet bed in the red
basket.
He fit the big basket in his van.

9

Bud got a tan box.
In it, Bud set a pet tub.
Bud fit the tan box in his van.
It sat on the red basket.

Bud fit a pet pen in his van.
Rex, his cat, was not in it.

Bud fit a bag in his van.
The bag had jam.
It had ham.

Bud had a big, big fan to fit in his van.
Did it fit?
Yes, Bud fit a lot in his van.

Bud is in his van.
Will it run?
It will not!
Sad Bud did not get gas!

What's in the Sack?

Written by Jim Edwards

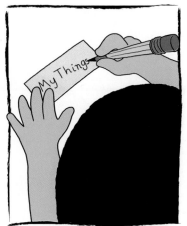

Short Vowels

Les	got	big	sack	well	can
add	tag	will	tell	is	in
fill	quick	fit	rock	on	hill
lock	dad	kid	pink	gum	pack
box	bell	ring	it	picnic	

Final -ck, -ng, -nk

sack	lock	pack	rock	pink	ring

High-Frequency Words

will	what	when	things
that	have	fun	

Les got a big sack.
Les can add a big tag.
That big tag will tell Les
what is in his big sack.

Les will fill his sack quick and well.
When can Les fit things
in his big sack?

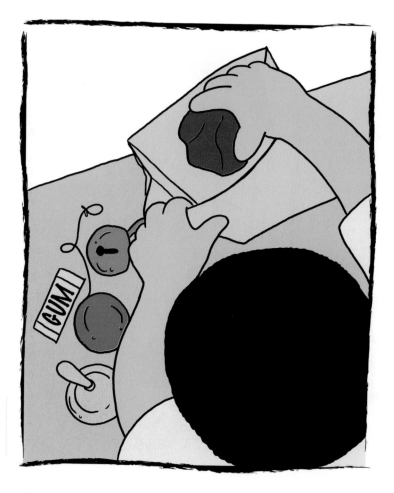

Les had a red rock.
Les got it
on a hill.

Les got a big lock
in his sack.
Les can pack quick.

Les got pink gum
in his big sack.
His pal got that
in a big box.

16

Les got a bell
in his big sack.
His bell can ring.
Les can ring his bell well.

Les can fit it
in his sack.
Les will have fun on his quick picnic.
18

Ike and Ace

Written by Harry Doyle

Long Vowels Spelled Vowel_e

mice	age	make	home	nice	safe
cage	fine	Ike	Ace	quite	wise
poke	nose	game	reptile	rose	ate
bite	cute	race	face	life	made

/s/c, /j/g, /z/s

has	mice	is	nice	age
cage	Ace	wise	his	nose
rose	race	face		

High-Frequency Words

it	good	at	her	age
make	every	small	home	

19

Tess has pet mice.
It is nice at her age.
The mice make a home in
a nice, safe cage.

20

Tess will add a fine mice bed for
Ike and Ace.
Tess has a lid.
Tess is quite wise.

Tess can see her big mice.
Ike can poke up his nose.
Ace can make a fun game.
Ace will act like a reptile.

Tess will put fine pellets
in their red pan.
Ike and Ace rose up
and ate every bite.

23

Ike is big and can not sit up.
Ace is small and cute.

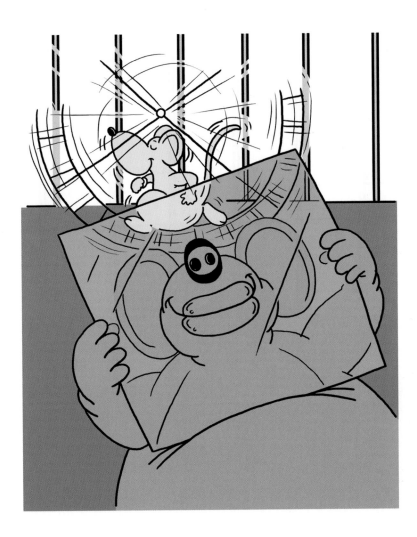

Ace is quick.
Ace can run in a race.
Ike can sit still
and make a face.

Ike and Ace have a fine life.
What luck for mice!
Tess has made a safe
home for Ike and Ace.

Pete Can Bake

Long Vowels VCe

Pete	bake	nice	cake
wide	tape	save	made
lime	cute	face	huge
nose	mistake	yikes	

High-Frequency Words

make	machine	it
face	huge	

Pete Can Bake

Pete can bake.
Pete can bake a nice cake.
Pete can sell a nice cake.

Pete has a box machine.
His machine will get a wide box.

27

It will get a cake.
It will set a cake in the wide box.
Then it will tape up the wide box.
His machine can save Pete work.

Pete made a nice lime cake.
His lime cake had a cute face on it.
It had a huge nose.
Pete made his lime cake fun!

Then his machine had to work.
But it made a mistake!
It did not get a wide box.
But it did get the nice lime cake.
It did tape the nice lime cake.
The cute face had tape on it.
The huge nose had tape on it.

Yikes! Pete had a lime cake mess!

We Can Do a Lot

Written by Victor Ramirez

Long Vowels Spelled Vowel_e

make	home	huge	Jane	face	use	nice
page	Dave	Kate	like	game	rule	base
invite	race	ride	bike	quite	bake	fine
cake	made	Rose	Mike	take	hike	age

/s/c, /j/g, /z/s

his	huge	face	use	nice
page	is	race	Rose	age

High-Frequency Words

huge	rock	work	machine
draw	face	color	

29

Tom can work
on his big machine.
Tom can make a home.
Tom can pick up that huge rock.

30

Jane will draw his face.
Jane will use a nice color.
Jane can fill a page with
his face.

Dave and Kate like that game.
Dave can tell us the rule.
Kate can help us get on base.
We can win!

Dave will invite Peg to race him.
Peg will ride on a bike.
Peg is quite quick.
Peg will win the race.

33

Dad will bake a fine cake.
Dad will sell it.
Dad made a huge
cake for Miss Rose.

Mike can take a long hike.
Mike can hike up the big hill.
Then Mike can hike back.
Mike will hike on rocks.

I like to sing.
I can sing well
at my age.
Can I sing a nice song?

On Stage

Written by Amy Thornton

Consonant Blends

and	stop	plan	glad
stage	strong	plastic	prop
black	mask	strap	act
skit	ask	clap	next

High-Frequency Words

sun	not	out
hot	of	front

The sun is not out.
It is not hot.
It is wet.
It is a sad time!

Max and Mel stop
and make a nice plan.
It will make
Mom and Dad glad!

Max can make a stage.
It is wide and strong.
Mel can make a plastic prop.
She will make the prop sit on stage.

Mel has a wig.
The wig is black.
Max has a mask.
He will strap it on.

They will act in a fun skit.
Mel can ask Mom and Dad
to sit in front of the stage.

Mel will sing a song.
Max will tell a joke.
Mom has fun.
Dad can clap a lot.

Max and Mel are a big hit!
Next time the sun is not out,
they will act a second time.

Fran and Flip

Consonant Blends

Fran	Flip	slept	left
plastic	felt	quilt	went
step	past	desk	jump
drape	snug	spot	grin

High-Frequency Words

of	felt
not	well

Fran has a cat, Flip. Flip has a lot of fuzz. Flip is a fuzz mess!

Fran slept. Flip left his plastic basket and hid. Flip felt it was fun to hide. But Flip did not hide well.

As Flip left his basket, fuzz fell on the quilt. As Flip went on the step, fuzz fell. As Flip ran past the desk, fuzz fell.

Flip made a jump to a sill. Fuzz still fell. Flip hid in back of a drape. Flip felt safe and snug.

Fran woke up. Fran did not spot Flip, but Fran did spot fuzz. It was on the quilt and the step. It was next to the desk.

At the drape, Fran did spot Flip. The fuzz mess just slept. Fran had to grin.

Can Ben Skate?

Written by Janis Lee

Consonant Blends

felt	skate	must	ask
went	Fred	best	help
static	strap	stop	fast
and	skills	glide	slide
smile	brave	pride	glad

High-Frequency Words

felt	well	must	said
mother	build	one	father

Ben felt sad.
Ben did not skate well.
"It must be fun," Ben said.
"I will ask Mom if I can."

48

Ben went to ask his mother.
"Mom, can I skate?" Ben said.
"We will ask Fred Fox," Mom said.
"Fred can skate best."

Fred Fox will help!
Ben got an ice skate.
His skate had a long lace.
It had static.
50

"Strap it on," Fred Fox said.
"You must stop fast
and use fine skills on ice."

Ben and Fred got on ice
to glide and slide.
Ben fell one time
but got back up fast.

52

His father came late.
Dad gave a big wave.
Dad had a smile on his face.

"I love to ice skate!"
brave Ben can yell with pride.
Ben is glad.
It is fun to skate well.

Lifting

Written by Paula Alvarez

Ending -s, -ed, -ing

dropped	lifting	makes
grabbed	helped	yelled
lifted	wiped	smiling
smiled	added	rested

High-Frequency Words

see	in	an
hole	day	now

Cam Clam dropped in
to see Clive Crab.
Clive makes his home
in an odd hole in a nice pond.

"Cam," said Clive,
"I am glad you came.
Can I get help
lifting this big box?"

"Lifting it will not be bad,"
Cam said with pride.
"I lift my home every day.
It makes me quite strong."

Cam bent and
helped Clive grab his box.

"Help lift," yelled Clive.
Cam and Clive lifted at the same time.
Up came his big box.

60

Cam helped Clive set the box
on his bed.
Clive wiped his face.
"Good job," Clive said, smiling.

Cam smiled back at Clive.
"Now we can rest," Cam added.
Clive and Cam sat and rested
in his snug hole.

Stan and Bev

Inflected Endings

rested	spotted	jumped	yelled
raced	steps	sitting	running
grinning	dropped	hopping	hopped
yelled	picked	smiled	

High-Frequency Words

jumped   up   from

As Stan rested on his grass, he spotted a red and black thing. Stan jumped and yelled, "Snake!"

Stan raced up the steps. Then he spotted Bev sitting on his deck. "Stop running. It is fake," Bev said grinning. Bev had dropped the fake snake on Stan's grass.

Stan sat back on his grass. He was glad the snake was fake. Then Stan spotted a huge black bug hopping at him. "That fake black bug is from Bev," Stan said.

The fake black bug hopped on Stan's leg. "That is a nice trick, Bev," yelled Stan.

Bev came and sat next to Stan. Bev picked up the black bug.

"Stan, the black bug is not fake," Bev said.

Stan jumped and raced up the steps. Bev smiled. "But the black bug is nice," Bev yelled.

Showing and Telling

Written by Terrance Saunders

Decodable Practice Reader 4C

Ending -s, -ed, -ing

jumped	wiped	running
dropped	hugged	lifted
jogged	hopped	smiled
asked	smiling	nodded
grinned	filled	pets

High-Frequency Words

jumped	up	early
ran	eat	from

Len jumped up early
from his bed.
Len wiped his face
and ran to eat.

66

"Stop running," Mom said.
"You will not be late."
Len sat and ate
eggs that Mom made.

Len dropped his stuff
in his big black bag.
Len hugged his mom.
He lifted his bag.

Len jogged up the lane
and hopped on his bus.
His bus came to a stop.
Len ran to class.

Len smiled at Pat.
"Did you bring it?" Pat asked, smiling.
Len nodded yes.
Pat and Len grinned.

Len got his bag.
In the bag was an odd cage.
It was filled
with five pet mice.

Len pets his mice.
Len kept his pets
with him in class.
72

Will the Whale

Written by Allison Fisher

Decodable
Practice
Reader

5A

Consonant Digraphs *ch, tch, sh, th, wh*

white	whale	fish
splashing	with	then
splash	when	this
ship(s)	shrimp	that
match		

High-Frequency Words

let	me	tell	white
about	by	friend	

Let me tell a tale
about Will the white whale.
Will is as big as a bus,
but he is quite nice.

Will is not a fish,
but he swims like one.
He likes swimming on his
back and splashing with his fin.

Will likes jumping up.
Then he makes a huge splash.
Will has fun gliding
on the wide waves.

When the wind
stopped and this ship got
stuck, Will helped.
Will pulled it to the dock.

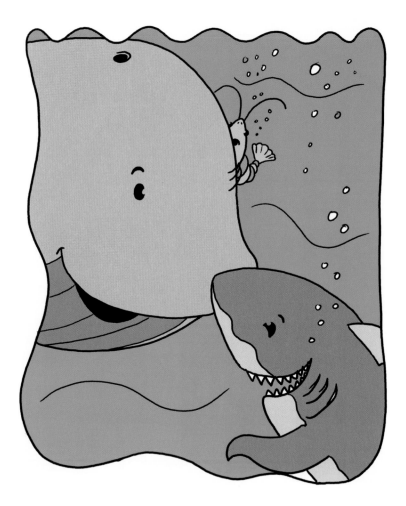

Sid the Shrimp is
his best bud.
Big Will hides Sid from
big hunting fish.

Will got a friend that
is a fine match.
His name is El.
Will is glad that he met El.

Will and El splash
side by side.
They wave to ships
that pass them.

Chet Checks

Consonant Digraphs

Chet	things	finish	shell
shrimp	trash	shelf	bench
pitch	catch	with	Beth
finished	shelling	white	checking
shopped	itch	pitching	catching
sixth	fresh		

High-Frequency Words

white   one   you

Chet Checks

Chet kept a list of things to finish. It
had five things.

1. Help Mom shell shrimp.
2. Shop with Dad and get lunch
stuff.

3. Set trash out.
4. Dust shelf and bench in den.
5. Pitch and catch with Beth.

When Chet finished shelling shrimp, he grabbed his white pen with red ink. It was his checking pen. Chet made one check next to "Help Mom shell shrimp."

Later Chet checked that he had shopped. Then Chet checked that he set the trash out and dusted in the den. Dust made Chet's nose itch.

Pitching and catching with Beth was fun. When he had finished, Chet checked it on his list. As Chet made his check, his pen ran out of ink. "You must add a sixth thing to that list," said Beth, "Get a fresh pen!"

Shane's Itch

Written by Renée McLean

Decodable Practice Reader

5C

Consonant Digraphs *ch, tch, sh, th, wh*

Shane	chased	bush
when	itch	scratched
chin	shin	chest
that	itching	

High-Frequency Words

had	came	gone	some
should	through	there	you

83

Shane chased his pup Spot.
Spot had gone through a shrub.
When Shane came out,
he had an itch.

84

Shane had an itch
on his nose.
Shane scratched it.

Shane had an itch
on his chin.
Shane scratched it.

Shane had an itch
on his shin.
Shane scratched it.

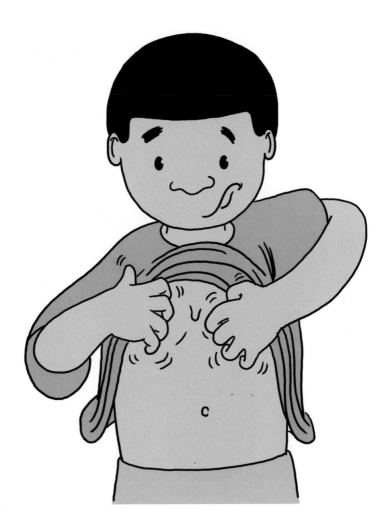

Shane had an itch
on his chest.
Shane scratched it.

His mom dabbed some
wet and pink stuff on his itch.
That itching stopped at last.

Mom said, "Shane,
some plants can make
you itch. You should
not go back there."

Farm Chores

Written by Andrea Erwin

Decodable Practice Reader 6A

R-controlled *ar, or, ore, oar*				Syllables VC/CV	
Darling's	farm	before	far	Patrick	rabbits
more	barn	roared	horses	Darling's	
Darling	porch	hard	chores	Darling	
part	sore	arm	dark	kitten	

High-Frequency Words

went	this	before	far
much	more	do	

Patrick went to Jon Darling's farm.
Patrick had not gone
to this farm before.
"Is it far?" Patrick asked.
"Not much more," Mom said.

Patrick spotted Jon's farm.
"His farm has a big red barn!"
Patrick roared.
"Are there horses, mules, and pigs?"
His mom grinned.

Jon Darling sat on his porch
with his kitten.
Patrick jumped out.
Patrick ran up to Jon.

"Are you set to work hard?"
Jon asked.
"We do chores on this farm."
Patrick will do his part
as well as he can.

95

Patrick swept pens.
Patrick fed chicks and rabbits.
Jon fixed his barn.

Jon Darling stretched his sore back
and patted Patrick's arm.
"You did a nice job," Jon said.

When it got dark,
Patrick went home.
"That was fun!" Patrick said.

Bart's Chore

Vowels: r-Controlled _ar, or, ore, oar_

farm	Bart	hard
chore	cart	barn
store	corn	Mort
barking	soared	short
dark		

High-Frequency Words

hard   went

Mom and Dad had a farm. Bart had one hard chore on that farm. He had to take a cart with corn to the farm's barn. Mom and Dad store corn in that barn.

Bart had a dog named Mort. Mort went with Bart on his chore

to take corn to the barn. Bart just got to the barn when Mort started barking! A robin had soared at his corn cart! Mort did not like that robin. Bart gave Mort a big smile.

The robin liked corn. Bart dropped bits of corn on the short path for that robin. The robin ate the corn while Bart and Mort got the corn cart in the barn.

The corn was safe in the barn. Mort did his chore! Then it started to get dark. Bart and Mort went home.

For the Family

Written by Marcie Watson

R-controlled *ar, or, ore, oar*

hard	for	roar
car	yard	horse
porch	jars	darling

Syllables VC/CV

baskets
darling
kitten

High-Frequency Words

hard	still	I
listen	heard	once

It is hard sitting still.
Dad is getting
a gift for us.
"I will listen for the roar of
Dad's car," Brett said.

Brett heard Dad's car
while sitting in his yard.
Brett rushed in at once.
What gift had Dad gotten?

"Can I see it?"
Brett begged.
"What can it be?"
Dad asked.

Is it a rocking horse?
Is it a porch swing?
Is it jars of jam?
Is it plants in baskets?

Dad yanked that box close.
"Time for this gift!" Dad said
with a quick wink.

106

Brett yanked off the string.
Brett lifted the lid.
It is a darling kitten!

Brett petted his kitten.
Brett is glad that
Dad got this gift.

108

Jem Wasn't Happy

Written by Stephen Lewis

Contractions n't, 's, 'll, 'm

didn't	I'm
isn't	let's
it'll	

High-Frequency Words

full	does	yard	bones
my			

Jem liked her dish.
Jem liked her yard.
Jem liked her bones
and fun things.

110

But Jem didn't act glad.
Jem moped in the yard.
Jem is not well.

Jem is my best pet.
I'm sad for Jem.
This isn't like Jem.

"Let's get to the vet," I said.
Jem went to a nice vet.
"If Jem is sick,
this vet can help."

That vet checked Jem.
"Jem isn't sick," she said.
"Jem is just sad.
Does Jem have friends?"

"It'll help if Jem spends
more time with pups," the vet said.
That vet had me
take Jem to the park.

Jem had lots of fun at the park.
Jem ran with pups and made lots
of pals.
I'm not sad for Jem.

Let's Wish

Contractions

can't	didn't	that's
I'll	let's	wasn't
it'll	Dad's	that's
I'm		

High-Frequency Words

yard   she   have

Barb and Dad sat in the dark yard. Dad spoke. "See those stars, Barb. Make a wish."

Barb had lots to wish for. "I can't pick one wish yet," she said.

Then Barb started thinking about Gramps. Barb didn't see him much.

"That's it! I'll wish for Gramps to visit us," Barb yelled.

Dad grinned as Barb made that wish. "Let's hope this wish works!"

That next morning, Dad yelled, "Barb, I see a big wish in the yard!"

Barb hoped this wasn't just a joke! "It'll make me sad if Dad's joking," Barb said.

Dad wasn't. Gramps was standing next to a cab and waving at Barb. "That's nice wishing, Barb!" Dad spoke with a grin.

Barb grinned back. Dad must have planned this visit. "I'm just glad Gramps came," yelled Barb.

It's Stuck

Written by Dan Arche

Contractions *n't, 's, 'll, 'm*

it's	let's
that's	can't
I'll	hadn't
wasn't	

High-Frequency Words

run	second	sure
either	off	laughed
they	great	

119

Liz and Brad gazed up.
"A cat is sitting on that second
branch," Brad said.
"It's stuck," Liz added.

120

"Let's run and tell Dad," Brad said.
Those kids ran five blocks.
Dad was sitting on his porch.

"There is a cat that's stuck,"
Liz said.
"It can't jump off the branch."
"Will you help?" Brad asked.

"I'll help," Dad said.
Dad, Liz, and Brad went back
to that sad cat.
It hadn't left that branch.

"Can you get it?" Brad asked.
"I sure can," Dad bragged.
"I'll either stretch up
or stand on that big crate."

Dad did his best.
Dad stretched up.
That cat jumped off!
That cat wasn't stuck!

125

Liz and Brad laughed
as they went back home.
"You're still great, Dad,"
his kids added.
126

Herb Helps Out

Written by Shanna Marcus

R-controlled *er, ir, ur*

Herb's	bird	Herb	her
first	third	stirred	stir
shirt	stirring	turned	

Syllables VC/CV

butter	batter
better	after
until	

High-Frequency Words

like	saw	put	also
first	into	done	

127

Herb's mom was making
a cake shaped like a bird.
Herb was helping.
He liked making this cake.

Herb's mom needed butter
for her cake.
She asked Herb to get it for her.
Herb got his bench first.

Herb had to stand on his bench.
He saw butter in the third box.
Herb got the butter for Mom.

130

Herb's mom put milk and
eggs in the batter.
Herb also helped get those things.

Herb helped stir the batter.
At first Herb stirred fast,
but he got spots on his shirt.
Herb got better at stirring.
He did not stir fast after that.

Herb's mom put the batter
in her bird pan.
She turned her clock.
It would take until five.

When the cake was done,
Herb and Mom made it into a bird.
It made Herb's dad smile.

134

Fern's Pitch

Vowels: r-Controlled *er, ir, ur*

Fern	Herbert	Church	Kirkville
Termites	hurt	Curt	Ferber
first	dirt	hurls	curves
swerves	burns	purses	jerks
bursts	twirls		

High-Frequency Words

first	fast
toward	into

The game is starting. Fern
Herbert will pitch for the Fort
Church Cubs. In this game,
they face the Kirkville Termites.
Kirkville's fans kid Fern and make
jokes. Kidding and jokes can't
hurt Fern.

135

Curt Ferber is the first Termite to bat. Fern rubs her hands in dirt. Then she hurls her first pitch. It curves and swerves. Ferber misses for strike one.

Next Fern hurls a fast pitch. As it burns past, Ferber swings for the second strike!

Ferber is mad. He purses his lips. Will he hit Fern's next pitch?

Fern jerks her arm up and hurls. Her pitch bursts from her hand and twirls toward Ferber. Curt Ferber swings and misses by a lot! Strike three!

Fern grins into her mitt. It will be a hard game for the Termites!

Curt's Bike Trouble

Written by Amanda Hopkins

Decodable Practice Reader 8C

R-controlled *er, ir, ur*

Curt	turned	swerve	dirt	curb
Curt's	hurt	Fern	Nurse	Kirk
hurting	perked	first		

Syllables VC/CV

corner
plaster
better

High-Frequency Words

time   ago fast   corner
toward say enough

137

Some time ago,
Curt rode his bike fast.
He turned at this corner
and rode toward a big hole.

138

Curt did not swerve.
His bike hit that big hole.
Curt fell hard in the dirt
by the curb.

Curt's leg hurt.
Fern helped him.
She yelled for Curt's dad.

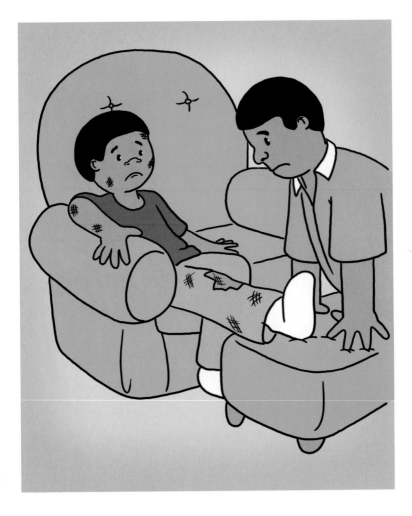

Dad was sad for Curt.
Dad had asked Curt
not to ride fast.
Curt didn't say a thing.

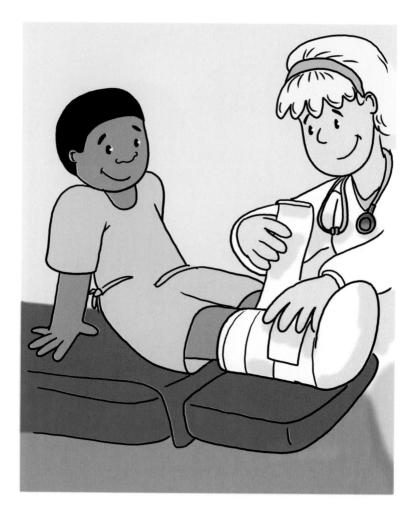

Dad drove Curt to see Nurse Kirk.
She put a plaster cast on his hurt leg.
It stopped hurting.
Curt perked up.

Curt went back to Nurse Kirk.
"This leg is better," Nurse Kirk said.
"You must use the rules
and not ride fast."

"I will ride well,"
Curt said.
"I had that big cast on
for long enough!"

Things to Do

Written by Tina Johannsen

Decodable Practice Reader 9A

Plurals -s, -es, ies, change f to v

places	things	lots	lunches	notes
passes	bases	stands	tunes	classes
puppies	leaves	crafts		

High-Frequency Words

are	together	go
give	won't	after

Fletch and Fran are pals.
They do things together.
Fletch and Fran go places
and see lots of things.

146

At lunch, Fletch and Fran
trade sack lunches.
Fran's dad packs snacks.
Fletch likes them.

Fran and Fletch give nice notes.
Fran hopes Fletch passes his test.
Fletch tells her about a fun plan he
has.

148

Fletch hit a home run.
Fran is glad.
When Fletch runs bases,
Fran likes to sit in the stands
and yell for him.

Fran got a prize for singing.
When Fran sings tunes,
Fletch won't miss it.
He thinks her singing is nice.

Fletch's mom drives them
home after classes.
They do work for class.
Then they spend time in the park.

Fletch and Fran visit with
puppies at the park.
They grab stuff
and make crafts.
Fletch and Fran have fun.

Yard Sale

Plurals

boxes	shelves	benches
glasses	dishes	dresses
books	brushes	waxes
crutches	sales	parties
pennies	dimes	

High-Frequency Words

people   after   bought

Mom and Dad had a yard sale. Dad got boxes of stuff from attic shelves. One box had an odd red jar. "We will use this for cash at the sale," said Dad.

At nine in the morning, Mom and Dad set sale stuff on benches in the yard. The benches had glasses, dishes, dresses, comic books, brushes, waxes for cars, used crutches, and much more.

At ten, the yard was filled with people. Dad and Mom had fun with them. "Yard sales are like parties," said Dad.

After five, Dad's red jar was filled with pennies, dimes, and more. People had bought a lot. Then a man spotted Dad's red jar. "Is that jar for sale?" he asked.

Dad dumped the cash in a bag and said, "Yes!"

Mom and Dad had a great yard sale!

Stan's Notes

Written by Joshua Blake

Plurals -s, -es, -ies, change f to v

lunches	buddies	notes
cards	elves	dishes
takes	tells	stuffs
slips	switches	lamps
things		

High-Frequency Words

probably	people	remember
bought	door	seemed

155

Stan forgets his lunches.
Stan forgets his bag.
His buddies are
probably sad for him.

It isn't fun to forget.
"People remember better
with notes,"
Stan's mom said.
She bought cards
and made notes for Stan.

It seemed like elves left notes.
This note on his cup
tells Stan to put dishes away.
Stan takes them to the sink.

This note at the sink
tells Stan to grab lunch.
Stan stuffs his lunch
in his bag.

This note on the clock
tells Stan to grab
his big bag.
Stan slips it on his back.

This note by Stan's door
tells him to flip these switches.
Stan turns off lamps.

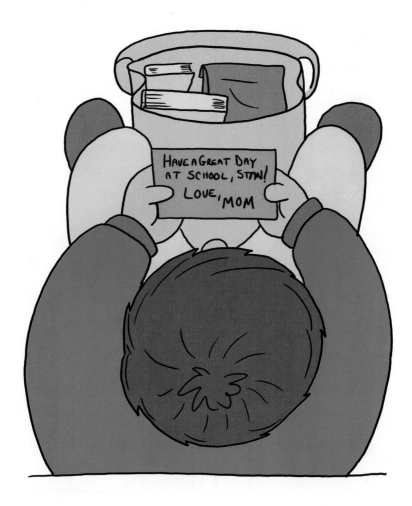

This is a big day for Stan!
Stan did not forget things—
thanks to Mom's notes.

Stay Away, Bugs!

Written by Julie Walsh

Decodable
Practice
Reader
10A

163

Bert is a nice horse.
But Bert does not like bugs.
Bert's main problem is
that bugs like Bert.

164

On hot days, bugs visit Bert's barn.
Bugs get on Bert's back.
Bert yells, "Scram!"
but the bugs stay.

165

Bert swishes his tail.
Those bugs think Bert
wants to play with them.
How will Bert make them go?

166

This makes Bert mad.
He uses his brain
to come up with a basic plan.

167

Bert fills a big pail.
He raises it up.
Then Bert waits for the bugs.

Bert raises his tail.
He swings it hard at the pail.
Splash! Bert got a nice bath,
and those bugs got wet.

169

Now the bugs stay away.
That's how Bert likes it.

Critter Trail

Vowel patterns *a, ai, ay*

rained	April	Jay	Gail
waited	trail	explained	wait
exclaimed	main	plain	play
quails	hay	gray	snails
paying	stayed	away	tail

High-Frequency Words

wait	minute
brought	main

It had rained and rained in April! Jay and Gail had waited long to hike. May first was a perfect hiking day.

Jay gazed west. "I say hiking the west trail is the best way," explained Jay.

171

"Wait a minute!" exclaimed Gail. "April rain brought roses to the main trail. That west trail is plain."

"Then on the main trail, you must play *Spot That Critter*," Jay said.

That's what Jay and Gail did on the main trail. Jay and Gail spotted five quails, a horse munching hay, five gray snails, and six birds paying a visit to a hole filled with rain. Jay and Gail stayed away when they spotted a white and black tail. It was a skunk!

"I can spot one more critter," smiled Gail after hiking. "You, Jay!"

Jay grinned at Gail's joke.

The Way to Play

Written by Jessica Twining

Long *a* Spelled *a, ai, ay*

Caleb	wait	playing	way
say	plays	day	rained
play	may		

Syllables V/CV

Caleb
behind
began

High-Frequency Words

wait	thinks	brought
minute	would	

Caleb likes to hide and wait.
Caleb likes to jump up fast.

Caleb thinks it is fun
playing this way.
Mom and Dad say that it is not nice.
Caleb will not make buddies
if he plays that way.

One day Caleb hid behind his door.
When Kim came,
Caleb jumped out at her.
Kim got mad and started yelling.
Then Kim went back home.

When it rained next,
Caleb brought his best game
and asked Kim to play it with him.
Kim would not play.
Caleb felt bad.

Caleb sat for a minute.
"It is not the best plan
to jump out," Caleb said.
"It may make people mad at me."

"I'm sad about jumping out, Kim,"
Caleb said.
"I will not do it again."

Kim smiled.
"That's fine," Kim said.
"Let's play that game."

Our Reading Party

Written by Melissa Stevens

Long e Spelled e, ee, ea, y

reading	read	we	week	party	teacher
each	please	clean	need	team	be
easy	sweeping	Dee	Danny	Dena	cleaning
Steven	Jean	Lee	Peter	seats	feel
readers	treat	neat	eat	even	

Syllables V/CV, VC/CV

party	easy	Danny	Dena
Steven	napkins	Peter	even

High-Frequency Words

our	class	room	read
fact	got	again	

181

The kids in my class like reading.
We read and read.
In fact, we got a prize
for reading a lot.

This week we will have
a big party.
Our teacher gave
each kid a job.

"Please clean up this room,"
he said.
"We need to clean as a team.
It will be easy that way."

Dee is sweeping.
Danny is picking things up.
Dena is cleaning the glass.
Steven is dusting that shelf.

We bring things for this party.
Jean is bringing cups.
Lee is bringing plates.
Mike is bringing napkins.
Peter is bringing forks.

186

We sat in our seats.
"You must feel good!"
our teacher said.
"You are good readers.
This prize is such a nice treat."

We clapped.
Then we had neat treats to eat.
Our party was a blast!
We will read even more to win
again.

Lee Rakes

Vowel patterns e, ee, ea, y

Lee	leans	she	deep
leaves	jeans	green	trees
feel	feet	cleaning	sees
dreaming	steamy	windy	chilly
pretty	each	season	weeks
seems	very	breeze	leaf
neat			

High-Frequency Words

pretty   very   again

Lee leans on her rake. She is standing in a deep pile of leaves. Leaves cling to her jeans.

Raking leaves is hard, but Lee likes it. She likes it also when green leaves change color and drift off trees. She likes the feel of crisp leaves on grass. She likes crunching them with her feet.

Dad is cleaning screens by the shed. He sees Lee thinking. "Are you dreaming of past hot, steamy days or windy, chilly days ahead?" Dad asks.

"I'm thinking of how pretty these leaves are," Lee tells Dad. "Each season has nice days and weeks."

"That seems to be a very wise way to feel, Lee," Dad admits.

A breeze twirls a leaf from a tree. Lee starts to rake again. Dad grins. Lee is a neat kid.

What We Do

Written by Karen Junias

Decodable Practice Reader

11C

Long e Spelled e, ee, ea, y

we	three	easy	green	tree
leaping	leaves	funny	beans	beets
windy	Jean	Bree	team	Jean's
very	Bree's	silly	each	teacher
read(s)	story	he	leave	week
city				

Syllables V/CV, VC/CV

easy	funny
because	better
pretty	silly
story	village

High-Frequency Words

science	watched	because
won	very	pretty
town	shoes	guess

191

In math we added.
What is three plus three?
That is easy!
Three plus three is six.

192

In science we watched
green tree frogs
leaping on leaves.
Those frogs are funny.

At lunch we had
green beans or red beets.
I chose green beans because
I like them better.

194

After lunch we played games.
It was windy, and we went back in.
Jean and Bree played on my team.
We won!

In art we made masks.
Jean's mask is very pretty.
Bree's mask is quite funny.
Mine is just plain silly.

196

Each day, the teacher reads
us a tale.
This is a story about an elf.
He came to a town
and helped a man make shoes.

I guess we must leave for now.
Next week we will read about a
neat city and watch red robins.
I can't wait!

198

Sam's Stroll

Written by Julia Jameson

Long *o* Spelled *o, oa, ow*

old	most	gold	go
so	slow	stroll	road
boat	toad	hello	row
over	croaked	bold	robot
floated	cold	goat	no
told	open	strolled	

Syllables V/CV

robot
open

High-Frequency Words

old	farm	cat	different
most	across	pushed	

Sam is an old farm cat.
He sits on his porch most days.
Every day is the same.
Sam likes it that way.

200

But on this day Sam feels different.
The grass is green.
The sun is gold.
The soft wind is nice.

"It is time for me
to go," Sam said.
And so he did.
Sam went for a slow stroll
on the dirt road.

Sam saw a boat
with three mice and a toad.
"Hello!" yelled Sam.
"Can you row me over there?"

"Yes, we can,"
croaked that bold toad like a robot.
Sam floated across
the cold pond in that boat.

204

Sam hopped out.
An old goat was at the gate.
"May I open this gate?" Sam asked.
"No, I will do it,"
the goat told Sam.

That goat pushed it open.
Sam sat for a while
with the nice goat.
Then he strolled home.

Whoa

Vowel patterns o, oa, ow

go	roller	coaster	Joan
okay	roll	slow	over
low	told	so	going
below	float	moment	whoa
thrown	moaned	groaned	

High-Frequency Words

always   been   pushed

"Let's go on this roller coaster,
Kath!" Joan said.

Kath had always been afraid
of roller coasters. Still she said,
"Okay!"

As the roller coaster started to roll, it was slow. It went over a low hill. "This is fun!" Joan told Kath.

Kath didn't think so.

Next the coaster started up a steep hill. It was slow, but the coaster kept going up and up. Kath spotted people way, way, below. On top of the steep hill, the coaster seemed to float for a moment. But then it dove fast! Joan yelled, "Whoa!"

Kath didn't! As the coaster whipped back and forth, the girls got thrown and pushed from side to side. Kath moaned and groaned.

When the ride was over, Joan yelled, "Let's go again!"

Kath groaned.

Joan's Long Day

Written by Michael Carlson

Decodable Practice Reader

12C

Long *o* Spelled *o, oa, ow*

Joan	told	Joan's	old
goat	yellow	hold	showed
bowl	most	scolded	toast
glowed	opened	slow	go

Syllables V/CV

opened

High-Frequency Words

car	wash	school
always	answers	been

Joan asked,
"Is it time?"
"Hop in the car,"
Dad told Joan.

Joan's mom and dad drove her
to a farm.
Joan petted fat pink pigs
and an old gray goat.
She saw cute yellow chicks.
"May I hold them?" she asked.

Farmer Jed showed Joan
how to brush the horse.
"Grab a cube from the green bowl,"
Jed told Joan.
"Those are what she likes most."

Mom, Dad, and Joan
drove to an old shop for lunch.
"First wash those hands,"
Mom scolded.
Then Joan had ham and toast.

Joan's mom and dad drove to her school.
Her teacher told them that Joan always has good answers in math.
Joan's face glowed with pride.

They opened the door
and left for home.
It had been a long day!
Joan's tired feet went slow.

"That's the last stop!" Mom said.
"Let's go home
and eat dinner."

Bill's Birthday

Written by Molly Pizziferro

Compound Words

driveway	backyard,	riverbank	weekend
cannot	birthday	mailbox	someone
something	mailman	mailbag	

High-Frequency Words

river	smile	such
even	where	something

May visited Bill's home.
Bill is not in his driveway.
He is not in his backyard.
He is not in his seat.
Where is Bill?

May went to the river.
Bill was sitting
on the riverbank.
He seemed sad.

"Hello, Bill!" May said.
"Put on a smile!
It's such a nice weekend.
You cannot be sad
on a day like this!"

"This is my birthday," Bill said.
"I didn't even get a card."
A drop rolled
off his cheek.

"Have you checked?"
May asked.
"No," Bill said.
"Then how can you tell
that you got no mail?" May asked.

Bill and May went
to Bill's mailbox.
Bill had no mail waiting for him.
He turned to go back in his home.

"Wait," May yelled. "I see someone.
That mailman is running late.
He has something big in his mailbag!"
His bag is stuffed with cards and gifts for Bill!

Jon's Postcard

Compound Words

postcard	weekend	sunrise
breakfast	buttermilk	pancakes
streetcar	hillside	tugboats
speedboats	supermarket	oatmeal
cupcakes	subway	railroad
lunchtime	drumsticks	peppermint
teacup	cannot	

High-Frequency Words

never	park
river	where

Jon gets a postcard in the mail. He reads it.

Jon,

It's Sunday. My mom and I are at Gramps this weekend. I have never eaten so much! At sunrise, we had breakfast. I had buttermilk

225

pancakes. Then we rode an old streetcar to a hillside park by a river. We spotted tugboats and speedboats. We stopped in a supermarket where we grabbed oatmeal cupcakes for a snack. We ate them as we rode on a subway. It was like a railroad!

At lunchtime, we had chicken drumsticks. Mom had peppermint tea in a huge teacup. Next we—

The postcard has no more printing. There was no space left to print! Which pal sent it to Jon? The postcard does not say. Jon cannot tell. But that pal has made Jon want lunch!

A Backyard Birthday

Written by Eric Vincent

Compound Words

weekend	granddad	someone
riverbank	catfish	cannot
birthday	lunchtime	backyard
mailbox	driveway	everyone

High-Frequency Words

park	never	finally
caught	believe	everyone

Lee went to a park
this weekend.
He rode with his mom
and granddad.

That park was big and nice.
Lee saw someone fishing
on the riverbank.
"Let's go!" he yelled.

Lee and his granddad went fishing.
Lee had never been fishing before.
Finally, he caught an ugly catfish.
"I cannot believe how big
this fish is!" Lee yelled.

Three kids asked Lee
to play games with them.
His mom made yummy snacks
while she waited for him.

"Tomorrow is my birthday,"
Lee told his granddad at lunchtime.
"We are having a backyard picnic.
We will eat what Dad makes."

Today Lee saw birthday
cards in his mailbox.
His granddad drove up
in the driveway.

Then Lee had lunch
with everyone in his backyard.
It was a fun party.

Rose Flies Home

Written by Kyle Hickey

Long *i* Spelled *i, ie, igh, y*

bright	sky	I	try
spider(s)	fright	cry	tiny
finds	my	child	flight
fly	high	I'll	right
sight	I'm	flying	cries

Syllables V/CV

spider(s)
tiny

High-Frequency Words

bright	sky	fine
try	tiny	

235

It is a bright day.
The sunny sky is fine.
"I must try to get home on time,"
Rose said.

236

Rose sees a spider
on the crack.
It gave her a fright,
but she won't cry.

"Some spiders bite," she said,
"but this tiny spider is nice."
That spider strolls off.
Rose went on.

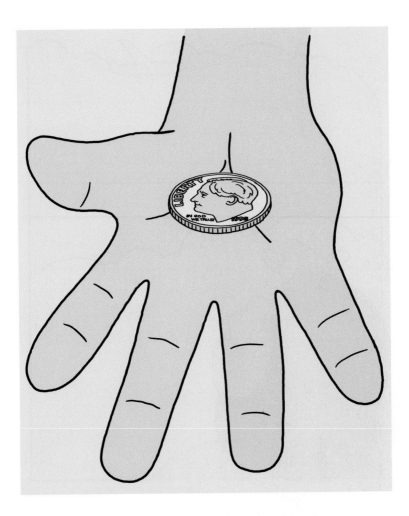

Rose finds a dime.
"For my bank," she said,
picking it up.
"I will save it for a treat."
The child went on her way.

Rose sees a plane in flight.
"Planes fly fast
and very high," she said.
"They must land on time."

240

Then Rose jumped and ran.
"Mom told me to be home
on time," she said.
"I'll run right home."

Her home is in sight.
Rose acts like a plane
in the sky.
"I'm flying home!" she cries.
She lands right on time.

242

Mike's Shirt

Vowel Patterns *i, ie, igh, y*

night	light	bright
finds	try	fights
tries	might	cries
sight	Tyler	right
why	replies	idea

High-Frequency Words

bright try believe

On the night of the class play, Mike has to dress in a red shirt. The light isn't bright backstage, but he finds his shirt.

On his first try, Mike can't get the shirt on! It's so tight! Mike fights and fights. He tries with more might. This try works. His red shirt is on, but it's still tight!

"My shirt feels tight!" cries Mike.

Mike's teacher tries not to smile. Mike is a funny sight in his tight shirt. Mike's teacher spots Tyler. His bright red shirt isn't right. But it isn't tight. It's big.

"I believe I see why that shirt is tight," the teacher tells Mike. "You have on Tyler's shirt."

"And Tyler has on mine," replies Mike. "I have an idea. Let's switch."

"That's a fine idea," his teacher tells Mike.

A Bright Child

Written by Daniele Wood

Long *i* Spelled *i, ie, igh, y*

bright	child	kind	find	spider
tiny	fright	I	by	myself
mind	right	night	sky	nightlight

Syllables V/CV

spider
tiny
before

High-Frequency Words

child	kind	don't
play	sometimes	their
many		

245

Kay is one
of three children.
Kay's age is half the age
of her big sister.
Kay is a bright child.

Kay is kind.
She finds a spider
and tells her sister,
"It's a tiny spider.
Don't give it a fright."

Kay likes to play
with her sisters.
"But sometimes I like to play
by myself," she adds.
248

"Dinnertime!" her mom yells.
Kay gets nice and clean
before she takes her seat.
That is a rule in their home.

Her mom asks her to
help clean.
"I don't mind," Kay thinks.
"It is right to help."

In the night sky,
Kay sees many stars.
She makes a wish on
one bright star.

Kay sees it is bedtime.
She sleeps by herself.
Her mom tucks her in
and leaves her nightlight on.

252

Faster, Colder, Brighter

Written by Steven Kaye

Decodable Practice Reader

15A

Comparative Endings *-er, -est*

faster	tighter	nicer	higher
saddest	happier	harder	colder
brightest	brighter	longer	happiest

High-Frequency Words

| city | too |
| way | store |

Kelly visited a big city.
"Cars go faster in this city
than at home," Mom said.

254

"People go much faster, too,"
Dad added as he stepped
out of a man's way.
Kelly held tighter
to Mom's hand.

They went to a store.
"This is a nice scarf," Kelly said.
"It's nicer than my old scarf."
"These prices are higher,"
Mom added.

They went to a park.
"That is the saddest duck,"
Kelly said.
"He would be happier
at our pond."

The wind started blowing harder.
"It's getting colder," Mom noted.
"We must go inside."
They went to a shop
that sold hot drinks.

After dark, the street lit up.
"Those are the brightest lights
I've ever seen!" Kelly said.
"It is brighter than day!"

"We cannot stay longer,"
Dad told them.
Kelly was glad.
"I like this city," she said,
"but I'm happiest at home."

Miss Camp's Funniest Faces

Comparative Endings –er, -est

nicest	funniest	smartest
brightest	happiest	silliest
sillier	hardest	meanest
meaner	greatest	

High-Frequency Words

city   too   question

The kids in Miss Camp's class feel that she is the nicest teacher in this whole city! And the funniest, too! Miss Camp feels that her kids are the smartest in this whole city. Each kid does well on tests. Maybe they are the brightest!

Miss Camp is happiest when her kids act silly. "I have a question, class," begins Miss Camp. "Can you make funny faces?"

"Yes," yells her class.

"Let's see the silliest faces you can make!" Miss Camp replies.

"Sillier!" yells Miss Camp. Each kid starts laughing. But Miss Camp laughs hardest.

"Now let's see the meanest faces you can make!" states Miss Camp. Each kid makes a mean face.

"Meaner!" laughs Miss Camp.

Each kid starts laughing. Then Miss Camp makes her meanest face. Miss Camp is the greatest!

The Longest Shopping Trip

Written by Julia Liu

Decodable
Practice
Reader
15C

Comparative Endings -er, -est

bigger	closest	biggest	nicer
longer	brighter	thinnest	thicker
happier	highest	finest	nicest
happiest			

High-Frequency Words

clothes	spot
hours	next
money	question

"My clothes don't fit!" Jake cried.
"You are bigger," Mom said.
"We will go shopping."

Mom parked in the closest spot
at the biggest store.
"This store closes in three hours,"
she noted.

Mom and Jake shopped for pants.
"These pants are nicer," Jake said.
"But those pants are longer,"
Mom added.

Next they shopped for shirts.
"Try that brighter shirt," Mom said.
"I like longer sleeves," Jake said.

Then they shopped for a coat.
"This is the thinnest cloth,"
Mom said.
"That thicker coat makes
me happier."

They shopped for shoes last.
"Those shoes on the highest shelf
are the finest," the clerk noted.
"We'll take them," Mom said.
She gave that clerk money.

Jake had only one question.
"Can we get snacks?" he asked.
Mom got them hot popcorn.
It was the nicest, happiest part
of Jake's day.

270